MW01142252

Women on Fire

by Irene O'Garden

A SAMUEL FRENCH ACTING EDITION

SAMUEL FRENCH

FOUNDED 1830

New York Hollywood London Toronto

SAMUELFRENCH.COM

ISBN 978-0-573-60318-1   Printed in U.S.A.   #25755

IMPORTANT BILLING AND CREDIT REQUIREMENTS

All producers of *WOMEN ON FIRE must* give credit to the Author of the Play in all programs distributed in connection with performances of the Play and in all instances in which the title of the Play appears for purposes of advertising, publicizing or otherwise exploiting the Play and/or a production. The name of the Author *must* appear on a separate line on which no other name appears, immediately following the title, and *must* appear in size of type not less than fifty percent the size of the title type.

In addition the following credit *must* appear in all programs distributed in connection with the Work:

**Originally developed and produced by
CHERRY LANE THEATRE,
Angelina Fiordellisi, Artistic Director**

WOMEN ON FIRE

Originally developed and produced by
CHERRY LANE THEATRE,
Angelina Fiordellisi, Artistic Director
Pamela Perrell, Director of Artistic Development

Women on Fire opened Off-Broadway in workshop at The Cherry Lane Studio Theatre, New York City, on October 14, 2003. The production then moved to mainstage at The Cherry Lane Theatre, opening on November 19, 2003.

Trude, Fern, Eileen, Clover,
Lydia, Miriam, Elizabeth, Rita,
Zatz, Kalisha, Audrey, Jordy.................Judith Ivey

Directed by..Mary B. Robinson
Stage Manager..Misha Siegal-Rivers
Set and Costume Design......................Michael Krauss
Lighting Design................................Pat Dignan
Sound Design..................................Bart Fasbender
Props...Faye Armon
Company Manager.............................Dave Batan
General Manager...Elliot Fox

CAST OF CHARACTERS

(Please note: Fire names have been used with slides of the character's names, but were not used in the NY production)

TRUDE—Tough Brooklyn photographer— fifties

FERN (*Hearth*)—hefty Midwestern housewife— late fifties, early sixties

EILEEN (*Coal Stove*)—Boston Irish, of great endurance—forties-fifties, rich lilt

CLOVER (*Conflagration*)—advertising exec, tough, crude and brilliant—fifties

LYDIA (*Smolder*)—dying manipulative Southern mother

MIRIAM (*Incinerator*)—animated, Jewish, Westchester clotheshorse—of "a certain age"

ELIZABETH (*Embers*)—feisty New England fighter, stroke survivor—sixties

RITA (*Campfire*)—musician, of great honesty— late forties

ZATZ (*Wildfire*)—edgy city kid—early twenties though seems younger

KALISHA (*Kiln*)—powerful black woman, physically strong—late twenties-early thirties

AUDREY (*Firestorm*)—passionate professor—forties

JORDY (*Fireworks*)—deeply delighted Appalachian dancer—nineties

To Judith Ivey—for her faith, her friendship and her finesse

TRUDE. (*On cellphone.*) Everything, Sam. Up in smoke. The fire didn't reach the house, but everything that mattered to me was in that studio. I could give a shit about the equipment, but all my negatives, all my prints. My Margaret Bourke-Whites. Thirty years of work. Spontaneous combustion, fire department said. I can't see how it happened. I'm a bulldog about chemicals.

I should never have taken that commission. If I'd been here, I might have saved something. But I was flying all over creation with this foundation thing, shooting Contemporary Women. Which I'd like to do. Most of the time anyway. I don't even know why they asked me. I shoot buildings, machinery, NASA, for chrissake.

I found a darkroom to print the rolls I shot on my trip. Wasn't expecting much. Took 'em telephoto. I didn't want to have to talk to them. You know women drive me crazy. But I gotta say there's interesting stuff developing in the trays. Not sure what to make of it. It's just, well... don't expect me at poker tomorrow. But don't give away my seat 'cause I'm coming to kick your ass next Friday night.

WOMEN ON FIRE

FERN. (*Sitting in a doctor's office, embroidering crewel-work.*) Oh, no, I'm not creative. I just like doin' crafty things. My hands gotta keep busy. Now, if I could bake in this waiting room you betcha I would! But these are portable. And it goes quick. I tried quiltin' once. It was depressing. Took too long to finish. I'll have these little kittens done before Doc even sees my bunions. They're goin' to a little girl I know. Oh, jeez! The kittens, not my bunions!

Oh, thank you. I like how the little stitches add up. Each one matters and you don't even know it. And it's like baking. You don't get an argument. You're only adding pleasure to the world. You're only going to make somebody smile. Unless of course, they're your daughter. Then you're just going to disappoint them no matter what you do. She lives in New York City. She's in publishing. Lord knows I can't bake for *her.* There's about one minute at Christmas where she'll eat something I make her, then all of a sudden it's New Year's. No butter, no flour, no sugar, no eggs. So now I bake for our funeral auxiliary. They like my cakes.You want something sweet, but not too sweet on a day like that.

Oh, yeah. So many families splittin' up. Parents move into homes, no friends come to mourn them when they die—they're too far away. So we keep an eye on the obituaries and we go. So they're not just layin' there all alone, you know. Least I'll have the funer-

9

al auxiliary to mourn me, cause I don't think my daughter'll come.
She's ashamed of me.

Oh, yes she is. Like kids when they're in high school, but she never
outgrew it. It's not just the weight. You shoulda heard her today. I
crocheted her up a little bathroom tissue cover cute as a bunny's
nose. She spends half the phone call jumping on me about taste. I
wanna say you're a fine one to talk about taste. You don't even eat.
But I bite my tongue. She says, "You could have been a fiber
artist," whatever that is. "A pastry chef." She's always after me to
become something. In my day you din't become something, you
were something. I wanna say, "Well you coulda been a wife if
you'da hung on to your husband." At least I did that much, even
though it wasn't any bed of roses. God rest his prickly soul. I'd like
to tell her there's one thing I want to be more'n any artist or chef.

But nobody can make theirself a gramma. You can only take the
first step and I did that forty years ago. And she don't count that as
an accomplishment. Jeez, if they only knew, right? None of this
creating's worth a peanut if you don't give it away. She don't know
that yet. She thinks it's all about getting stuff or doing stuff. All this
accomplishing just makes her cantankerous. And then she says—
Oh never mind.

That's why I like baking. No bickering. Everything always cooper-
ates. The eggs and flour and butter are always friendly to each
other. Your extracts and your spices get along fine. The pan don't
get sick of the batter. Dough never says, "Something came up
today—I couldn't rise. I forgot to turn golden brown." It never lets
you down.

I don't know where I went wrong with her. She's such a sourpuss. She's bein' what she says she wants to be, and the one thing I want to be I can't be. I pray about it. God makes me laugh. I know I shouldn't say it, but He makes wisecracks when I pray. Like today. I pray, "Oh God, please send me a grandchild." "Why?" He says. "So someone'll love me unconditional," I says. "*I* love you unconditional," He says. "Oh come on. I can't do you up a baby blanket or bake you sugar cookies. Please send me someone for *me* to love unconditional." "I already did," He says. "She lives in New York City, remember?" I pray, "Well then couldn't you send her a child so she'd know what I been through with her?" And He says, "Of course you want your kids to understand what havin' kids is all about. But do you really want *them* raisin' your grandkids?" Jeez, I had to laugh. We just gotta bite our tongues, don't we? We just gotta be as nice as butter and sugar.

EILEEN. (*Kneeling in the confessional.*) Bless me, Father, for I have sinned. It's been too long since me last confession. Before I get to me sins, I have a question. Do you have to make someone a promise just cause they're sick and they want you to? Isn't a deathbed promise the ultimate cruelty, Father? You've no right to try to exert your will beyond your time allotted, do ya? And when they're lying in their deathbed as long as she's been lyin' in hers, think of all the promises they could get from you. It's mean. It's a mean old thing from a mean old bitch. I mean person, Father, a mean old person who sucked away my life.

Never, I said. I'll flush your ashes down the toilet. Why should you die happy? You made us all miserable, you miser, you skinflint. Hardly let me pay the electric, even though the old man left you plenty. Next time they take your blood, I wanna see it, says I. I think it's green venom in there.

Oh, I know I'm bad, Father. But I'm hardly well meself. The very sheaths of my hands are worn. My skin feels all loose as if me bones were falling out. I see bracelets of light and spangles, me head's a helmet of agony. I'm ridin' the Ferris wheel of migraine, again, thanks to her.

No, I won't see the doctor for it. At least t'is my own. Me

headaches are my only privacy, Father. That and confessin'. So these are me sins: I've sinned against the fourth commandment more than I can count. But where's the commandment on honoring your children? It can't be right what she done to me. You seen her, Father. Laughing at me birthmark, calling me clumsy. I know I'm not pretty like me sisters or smart like me brothers, but she's squashed me confidence since I was a wee girl.

I try to hide it from her. You can't hurt me. I'm too soft, I tell her. You can slug a brick wall, but not a cabbage leaf. The leaf don't have it to give back. But the worst is, Father, she's made me unfit for any man, so's I'd have to tend her in her old age. I don't think I can forgive her.

It's more than a trespass, Father. Me future's passed me by. Even if I got me birthmark taken off, who'd want me temper and me tongue? She's trained that into me and now they'll be none to tend me in my old age. It's the same sad story. A broke spirit is nothing new, except it's mine.

She don't have much hope herself. Sometimes I yell at her to get a rise out of her. Is that a sin?

About this deathbed promise—She wants her ashes in her garden. I don't mind dumpin' em, but she wants me to keep care of her garden and her idiot cat. I don't like the outdoors, the muck and the bugs. I'd rather be watching the basketball game. She got me into that, you know—she loved how quick it was. To watch their bodies jumping, moving, sweating—she loved the very squeak of sneakers on the court. Course now she can't follow a game. She can't follow a raindrop down a windowpane. She can't follow a beer with a burp. I'm sorry, Father. I hate that I hate her. It's just the way she has to have the lights off, but then she has to have the heat up. Then I turn me back, she's drunk the *holy* water, Father. And the cat's almost worse than her for peeing all over the place.

Yesterday she's spouting nonsense about "Oswald! Oswald!" "Who's Oswald, you crazy bat?" "Oswald! Stole me rubies! Me rubies!" All day she's on about it. Then it occurs to me. I bring her the President's picture, and her little one of John-John salutin' the casket. That calmed her down. And the old scrapbooks. She gets an M&M for every face she recognizes. What a way to end a life.

So I confess the sin of pride, the sin of guilt, the sin of despair, except they all feel like penances to me. Not fun, like sin should be, eh, Father? And you might as well ask The Ladies' Auxiliary would they have a spare wheelbarrow and a spade? She's busted ours, you know. She mighta buried the old man's money out there, for all I know.

You got the sisters prayin' for me, don't ya?

Yes, Father. Thank you, Father. Same time tomorrow.

CLOVER. (*In therapist's office; her cigarette remains unlit.*) I love sex and I love riches. How's that for a lead? Can you tell I ran an ad shop for twenty years? Touch a match to my fine cigarette, won't you? I do confuse the two sometimes. Get turned on buying something.

Of course, creating that connection is—maybe *was* my business. Why they paid me riches. Which I may never see again. Riches which to me are black jade gold-flecked eggs slipped into an exquisite native basket. Riches which to me are the suede of a dear friend's arm I fly first class to stroke. Riches which to me are little bottles little baubles little bourbons in my life.

That's copy. No doubt you're after something else. Smoky thoughts, snappy thoughts. What else do I love? The smell of New York. Stink of work mixed with bus and hotdog fumes. That smell of power fires my blood and my fire streaks across billboards and busses and screens and magazines because I'm apex at The Ad Biz. Smell of fresh ink on a contract: sweeter than Paris in spring. And the smell of their fear when they think I won't sign. Smell of quaking balls, I call it. Love that smell.

When you buy what I sell you accept me. When I buy what you sell I'm a sucker. I'm hard to love, I know. Not that it really bothers

17

me—I don't have the time to connect. Occasionally I wind my liquored limbs into leopard lingerie and take to the clubs for a cityquick hump in a corner. I do love sex, after all. When you buy what I sell you accept me, so to speak. So why give up advertising?

There was this basket of thanks on my desk. Hefty lacquery basket, big enough for firewood. A thunderclap of vivid cellophane, filled with truffles, foie gras, pâté, and champagne. Those assholes knew me well. Campaign from hell, but done. You've seen it—brilliant concept—shooting high-end clothes on Death Row inmates. Haunting shots. Really.

So, this basket. Of riches. My pores opened, my juices ran. I never leave in the middle of the day, but I left in the middle of the day.

Sucker was so big I almost had to get a second cab. Hauled it up to my place. Opened it up. No one to really celebrate with—hard to love, you know…Still, a great thing, great triumph. Damn champagne was cold. That's class. Love class. Try to have fucking class. And I was just fine. I stuff half the stuff away, hadn't even opened the champagne yet—was gonna, but hadn't—and there's this little basket in the big one, a little cheap Chinese one they stuck the Twinings teabags in and you know I gotta tell you, I'm ashamed, but I gotta tell you, I thought *jeez they coulda gotta better basket than this chintzy Chinese thing.*

Here's this big beautiful basket and I bitch about that. You think I haven't gone over every thought I thought with a fine-tooth comb? And I take out the teabags and think I'll give this to my neighbor's kid for crayons or chocolate or whatever, and I swear by the deity formerly know as God, I hear this Chinese laughter, which I think maybe's a delivery next door, even though my neck is prickling.

And I see like I see you, slim fingers poke and pull the willow and I hear conversations I don't have: *How sons grow, how husbands complain.* I've been making products speak for twenty years, but not like this. *How soon till the peonies bloom?* Then I feel these feet like feet shoved inside of mine and then I feel my own feet strangling in Barbie shoes, actual size, it feels like. And I kick them off and make up a little rhythm jingle *My feet get the blues without comfortable shoes.* And then I think *their feet are bound.*

Then I don't want to think any more, so I pour the champagne, pass up the foie gras, cause I don't want to hear any screaming geese just now and I turn on my big screen, which mostly I don't watch but for commercials we make, and I start hearing Mexican workers assembling the set, sweating it out till Saturday night, so I turn it up to cover the sound, for chrissake I'm s'posed to be celebrating. And it's the middle of the day, right, so I see the kiddie commercials: teddy bears being run over; kids sullenly returning toys to Santa, demanding the product instead. Coke as the Mother Breast dressed as a Polar bear—a wordless commercial a *baby* can grasp.

Now, I admire this stuff professionally, but now I'm feeling sick, so I go out on my little balcony, get some air, and I look down and here's this procession of little kids, little Madelines, two by two holding hands, off on some little field trip and I hear this chainsaw, and what am I, going crazy? And I get this image, like how they clearcut trees, only it's these little kids, their trust, their humanity, we pulp it, blow our nose in it, throw it away. And I grip the railing cause I don't wanna throw myself off.

I always thought of culture as the body you grow up in. You get your share of pleasure from it. Sometimes it's a bother having one at all. But it's not like you can reject it. Good or bad, you're in it and you live with it, and if you're a good American, you profit from it.

But that day, this culture seemed like an awful infection I came down with, and I thought, I don't want to spread this anymore.

So I don't wanna go back over any childhood bullshit. I just need you to gimme some pills or tell me how the fuck to find another line of work. These side effects are fucking killing me.

LYDIA. (*Slumped in her sickbed with a glass of wine and a handheld tape-recorder.*) Darlin', I'm glad you decided to listen to this tape. I know I'm an unnatural mother, and before I die I've gotta explain why. No doubt I'll still roast in hell, but then I'll see your father over there in the stupid corner and that will give me pleasure for all eternity.

I tried so hard to make you what you are and I'm so proud of your success. I was fixin'to bust when I saw that motor-display down to the Bookatorium. I asked Earl to order me one. I'm gonna put it in your room.

I've been trying to think how what I done done done come about. I could say it's Margaret Mitchell's fault, it's William Faulkner and Truman Capote and Tennessee William's fault. But I don't know was it their fiction or their lives?

I only know in every biography of every great writer I ever read, you never hear of any loving upbringing. A writer gotta have drive, gotta have ghosts, gotta have drama to draw from.

Sometimes it's too much and it chokes them. It's very delicate to get the balance right. That's why I was tough on you, why nothing you did was good enough for me. You know from my card-playing I'm a manipulator. The only real talent I ever had. Not like you.

21

I know it was evil in me, pure ice-evil running in my veins and do not ask me how I could for so many years live with it. I know it's why I let the white wine tear my liver up.

I did not live the life I wished to live. I did not have the imagination it required, except where you were concerned. And I could imagine such a future for you.

I know you want to know why. I know you want to know what went on under my Papa's live oaks, around my Mama's kitchen table, behind the library door. I could tell you, but it wouldn't be near as good a yarn as you can spin. I don't wanna take that from you. I will say, stories are a damn good hiding place. But then, sometimes it's bad, what stories do. They show you how to do things people never should be doing.

I don't know what I thought was more important than a child's love. I expect I'll find that out some day.

I don't ask you to forgive me. I see myself turn up in your books often enough to know it's impossible. Just had to get it off my chest, and let you know you weren't crazy. Or if you are, it's my gift to you.

MIRIAM. (*Sharing a table at a lively bar.*) Darling, darling, no young man is worth it. I know just what you need. Drink
up. Let your Auntie tell ya a few things. The facts of life have their
place, but you'll enjoy the facts of shopping even more. I'll tell you
how it's done, but I'm not going with you. Properly done, shopping
is an intensely private act, if you know what I mean.

First, you gotta prepare, as careful as if you're having an affair. Oh,
I'm sorry. What I mean is: bath, powder, perfume. Detail makeup
in your magnifying mirror, tasteful earrings, a casual but elegant
outfit, and dark glasses. You can go into the city, but I find it dis-
tracting. I prefer a mall, specifically, The Crystal Goliath Mall.
They have it all. The parking fields can get a little confusing, and
sometimes I'd like to blow up all the cars and people except for the
salespeople, well, no, except for the *good* salespeople. What stops
me is then I'd be the only person shopping. I would not be anony-
mous. Didja ever read Erica Jong? Then you know what I mean by
a "zipless shop."

Besides there's all that weather in the city. At the mall, whatever
the chaos, you leave it in the airlock when the door slides shut. It's
like entering a lover's arms. Oh sorry, honey. What I mean is it's a
safe place. A clean place. And no one will say anything mean to
you.

23

To get the most pleasure, don't head for your favorite store right away. Work up to it, know what I mean? Is this sounding familiar? I start with Sears or Penny's. I love strolling through them. Maybe you never did this, but I used to passionately page through those catalogues, first for the toys, then for the bras, then for the white provincial furniture. Oh, that corner desk! Of course their merchandise offends me now, but that's why I go. To remind myself how far I've come.

Then you pass into the great halls of the mall itself. First, a fabulous little clothing shop: The Gilded Cheekbone. Take your time. Stroke the merchandise. Shopping is whoopee for the fingers, darling. Touch, fondle, drape luscious things over your nearly naked body. Not that I often try things on. I don't like a lot of hairspray and I don't like mussing myself. It's like when Abe kisses me right after I put lipstick on, you know? Oops—don't mean to bring up a touchy subject, dear. Two more daiquiris, please.

And the truth is—this is a matter of both pride and frustration to me—my taste is now so sophisticated I rarely find anything I actually want to buy. So now me and shopping are like Abe and flyfishing. He throws them all back. It's all in the hunt.

I do love to pet the clothes and talk to the designers. Oh I don't mean I talk with actual people. It's one of my shopping rules to speak as little as possible. But say I find a navy wool jacket with excellent gold buttons. I'll congratulate Liz Claiborne. "Good work, Liz," I say to myself. I don't buy her—except those peach jeans.

Thank you, my dear. Strawberry's here, banana's hers. Where was

I? Sooner or later though, a salesperson interrupts. Since I don't buy much, I find this irritating. Unless of course, it is that rare creature: the excellent salesgirl. I admit I am exacting in my standards, but having myself been sales help, I know the challenges and I know they can and should be met if our human bonds are not to break down altogether.

You wanna talk about a salesgirl? The other day I found the precisely most lovely and appropriate pink silk blouse. The silk itself had a glorious hand, but the coup de grâce was the color: the merest hint on the cheek of an antique doll was this pink. It was one of the few things I actually had to have. It fit and it felt like a dream.

The ax fell when I returned it to the padded hanger. There clear as day, along the shoulder, unmistakable: *shop soil.* Back to the rack. The last one. The salesgirl's a gem, just like you, just out of college, and though someone of her intelligence is undoubtedly pursuing another career, she conveys that her sole purpose is assisting me. That's the feeling we're shopping for. Her name is Lena. She has a great haircut, with bangs, asymmetrical, and a super sense of timing. "Great color," she says, like a friend, like a sister, who spontaneously appears. Then she quietly goes back to folding and fleck-picking the goods.

I had to ask the most dreaded question of all. "Pardon me, Lena. Would you have any more of these?" Most of the time help says "All we have is what's out," like it's a punchline to an unfunny joke. But good help, good help knows there are no more pink blouses and there never will be more pink blouses, but good help always offers a moment of hope, like a bonbon: "I'll be happy to look in back for you." Which Lena does.

Then here she is at my elbow. "I regret to say, you have the last one." I hold it up: "Shop soil, as you see. Definitely noticeable, like a fine sift of ashes." Lena sadly shakes her head. You'd think it was her mother's. "I'm so sorry." Where else you get a good apology these days? "We do take precautions, but sometimes it happens. If you really like it, you could have it cleaned and I'm sure we'd reimburse the bill. And knock five dollars off the price."

Now it's not bargains I'm after. That's vulgar, a cheap thrill, like paying for sex. Certainly the thrill of "Sale" can reach like a finger in the right place, so to speak, but your real sportsmanship is enjoying the sensuality with utter indifference to the outcome. "I'll take it," I said, and there is a rush, my dear, of blood right away to the face and the fingers—the big O of purchase, you know what I mean. *(Groaning orgasmically.)* Ohhhhh! Sweeter than taking it home. Now it's a prize. Soon it's a possession. Not unlike a husband, for your information. Then there's the rustle of tissue, the box. "I know you're going to be happy with this," she says, and I'm telling you, that's one of the main reasons to shop: because people know you are going to be happy and they tell you so. And you give them your card, and you're approved! They always approve me when I shop. Then the satisfying rattle of the cord-handled bag ascending and descending over the salesdesk. "We appreciate your coming in" says Lena. Oh, to be appreciated.

Call me shallow, darling. Shopping makes me more alive than anything.

ELIZABETH. *(In her garden.)* Why on earth have a vegetable garden? Grocery stores overflow with produce now. Not just stupid produce, like iceberg lettuce, but baby greens and baby carrots, baby potatoes, and baby bok choy. Have they been babied do you think? How can they be, drenched in the suffering of migrant workers? I undertook gardening in the sixties, as a political act, to remind myself of the tremendous invisible labor of producing food.

So I don't let just anyone come tramping around in here.

I don't grow much of any one thing. I can't grow a season's worth of peas—I'm not that interested in peas. Potatoes. Does it matter? Except that once a year, that sweet taste of the earth itself, the calm, the balance. How many salads do I really eat? Not that many from the dirty gritty garden, yet I tend them like the horticultural vestal virgin I am. They are my offerings. My vegetable garden is a ceremonial appreciation of Earth and her peoples, one of the most human things I do.

While I'm not indifferent to the harvest, it's the least interesting part of the process to me, a fact which revolts me, incidentally. It's unnatural for humans to be so affluent they don't care. What a culture. I give away what I can, but sometimes, like the lettuces there, I just let the plants fulfill the whole cycle.

Take a look here. Every time anyone gets a little prideful about human accomplishment, I hand them one of my tomatoes — Mortgage Lifter's my favorite—and remind them of the pink Styrofoam baseballs they get in the winter.

My garden began as a political act, and it is still a political act, but one spring evening a few years ago, beauty crowded out the politics. I was heaving shovels of bark mulch over my newly planted beds, and picking up double handfuls, tossing it down, spreading it out. The air was perfect, insects all minding their business, not bothering me; my body feeling joy in purpose, glad of work on earth in a way it never felt stuffing envelopes, making phone calls, picketing.

Hunger and sunset tell me it's time to stop and go in, but I don't want to. It's getting darker; at the same time it's getting lighter: a full pink moon rising up through the trees like the answer to a question. I'm still working. A tune pops into my head. I start singing, *(Singing to the tune of "I could have danced all night.")* "I could mulched all night". I'm caught up like a tingling girl of twelve. I'm falling in love with the earth, with plants and soil in the spring—a luscious obsessive harmless affair every year, as sensual and responsive as you could wish. Plants are utterly vulnerable, utterly sensual, open, awaiting you—

It wasn't just the pink moonlight—the vegetables really were as beautiful as flowers. There's democracy for you. Ever since, I'm not so rabid, working for justice. I think of working for beauty in the human garden.

I don't spend my life in the garden, you know. The plants become more independent in the summer. So do I. We function without one another's obsession. We bid adieu, each fall, which sweetens it, sweetens it.

So, the way I reckon, the stroke was just a touch of frost, and you're my burlap. Which means that in addition to the other chores, we will stuff envelopes, make phone calls, picket, because it must be done, same way I weed beneath the beating August sun.

RITA. (*Cross-legged at a campfire.*) I wasn't that young. Late twenties. Stable relationship, or stable as two people working out neuroses can be. Using an IUD. Then I was late. I know women who chart their periods chapter and verse—know the minute they ovulate, know their procession of hormones like men know a team coming out on a field. But I've been pretty regular, never gave it much thought.

So this was weird. I kept waiting for the jumpstart, all the way till next month. Still no period. Now I'm nervous, though I haven't told him, because I *couldn't be*, the IUD, you know, and why alarm him needlessly, but I better look into this.

Free Pregnancy Test. I copy down the number from the bus ad, afraid that "free" means free to listen to their diatribe on what I ought do, but thinking it might be worth sitting through since I could do this all without him knowing. No drugstore tests back then. They take my pee and blood; a smiley point-cap nurse comes back and puts me in the Doctor's office. He comes in and says, "Your test was positive." "Huh?" "You're pregnant. About 8 weeks along." I'm flabbergasted. "My God! How? I've got an IUD."

"Ten percent get pregnant anyway. Nothing's 100% effective. Do you know what you're going to do?" "Well, I know I won't be having it, there's just no way, we're not set up for this. But where do I go?" I was relieved they had no agenda. There was a dizzying discussion of trimesters meaning, "Soon. Do this soon." They gave me Planned Parenthood's number. I was in such a state of shock I took a cab. A baby in my body. Something I never thought I'd feel, I'd carefully planned not to. I felt a flickering like candleflame. I knew I'd never have this baby, and yet part of me was glad, honored that Evolution found me worthy, that my pipes were working right, the universe congratulated this with an embryo, no, *fetus* at eight weeks. A sorrow-coated joy.

He was as staggered as I. Not ten percent careless, or ten percent chancing. Ten percent corporate error, ten percent bad design, ten percent bad luck. He asked for information. I told him what I knew. He hugged me, and was sorry, so sorry. I couldn't expect any gladness from him; it was a problem to solve, but some part of me wanted him to be proud somehow, I don't know, I guess that we were grown-ups. I said I'd set it up; he said he'd come with me.

Over my pounding heart sounded a kind voice on the phone. "The soonest appointment we have is two weeks; come in before; we'll discuss the whole thing." I went. They described the vacuuming, the bleeding and the cramps. "Soon. Do it soon. Though you can decide that day not to do it." Of course, there was no question, no question—there was my work, there was his. We always said we never wanted children. We'd reproduce in music. And as for adoption, I once had a long conversation with a crazy writer who'd been in and out of foster homes. I could never subject a child to that. There was no question, no question. That was why I could let myself feel.

We decided to follow our plans to visit his folks in the country.

Smiles in their eyes, and discomfort in me, knowing I was turning off the road of their grandchildren, and they would never know. No chance of sharing a bed there. We hiked to a childhood spot he knew—up in the hills and off in the woods. We made love in the wintergreen—so fragrant. I have never had sex like it, before or since. Overlooking a wide green valley, body arched in pleasure, every cell, united not just with my lover, but all ages, all biology, my body bearing the physical point of sex, its one and only participation with the Darwinian purpose. I loved that little candleflicker for it.

That day, I quit smoking. Silly, but while it was in me, I wanted it to have the best of care.

Within a week, The Day arrived. Yes, I was afraid. This choice, this decision, this word was about to become a genuine bleeding cramping loss in *my* body. I have friends who chart medicine, chapter and verse, but specula and cannulas and gloves were cold and foreign to me and I was halting three probable lives. He did come along, and brought peonies. He would have taken on the pain if he could have.

The week before I found out I was pregnant, I bought and read a photography book called "Behold Life," with images of marvels of the microscopic world. I thought it cruel, cruel of the world to sharpen my appreciation then ask this of me. Yet, that's how I knew to whom I offered gratitude. I underwent the strange, uncomfortable, sorrowful, relieving experience. Yes it hurt, and I was conscious. I'd spent a good part of the previous summer learning Shakespeare's sonnets. I recited them to cover the vacuum sound, along with childhood prayers and song—I hated the sound of vac-

uums even as a child. My living flicker and I relinquished one
another.

I recovered, as I knew I would. It was the right thing, as we knew
it was. Our lives belonged to us. Every child has a right to be wel-
comed and loved. I would have resented a child who would have
asked my life of me. But I love my living flicker, who gave me the
gift of all biology like a bouquet and accepted its departure as a
peony its cutting.

ZATZ. (*Perched precariously with a spray can.*) Attention Shoppers! Is there a publisher in the house? Anywhere in this mega-ultra super-cyclopedic bookatorium? I'll get down off this bookcase when you bring me a publisher. And I'll spraypaint a book a minute until you do! Stand back! It's pointed at Moby Dick and I'm gonna use it! *(Pssss)* Bye-bye Ahab! Took your whole life to nail him, and I got him in two seconds. Melville to Hellville.

Don't try to pull a ladder up! I'll spray you fast as you can climb. You don't know what else I got on me. No, dickhead, I'm not using. Words are all I use, man. I roll 'em into sentences and smoke 'em, one after the other, shooting right out of my fingers sometimes. Sometimes tips of orange fire swell and glow and pull me forward. Or blue smoky thoughts which where are they leading me? How can I capture them? Sometimes I stub them out before they're halfway done. Words are so mysterious, man. And they're free! Use all you want, there's always more. A day without words is like...Zatz my point!

And Zatz my name. Z-A-T-Z Because the purpose of a writer is to point things out. *Zatz* it. *Zatz* me. And you will not forget me. Sinclair Lewis. To the sewers! No one reads you any more anyway. *(Pssss)*

I see you staring at my piercings, buddy. Unlike your sideburns, these *mean* something. Used to get one every time I got a reject slip. Had to quit it, as you can see. This tattoo's for my first published piece. *Crucified Armpits.* Story about this renegade butcher, Torn Jimmy, meets this Quaker hooker, Annie. It's good. Published in a 'zine out of Austin, Texas, called Rat's Ass, which this store won't even carry. Even though somebody wrote me a postcard that they liked it. Zatz what keeps me at in the bull's eye of this screwed rude world. *(Pssss)*

Did you know making messes is a crime unless it's someone's life you make a mess of? Not that I'll play you my xylophone of foster homes, houses of louses, except to say, whatever you do, don't injure objects. *(Pssss)* They'll lock me up for this. My life will go into another file. File, life, life, file. Cool. *(Pssss)*

Oooh, I hate her books. You know she doesn't care about her characters. *(Pssss)* Don't you think I improved her big display up front? Aw, we'll get her a cardboard sling, a little cardboard neck brace. Hard to tell her apart from cardboard. Zatz my point. I worry about *my* characters, my people. I hate even putting them into conflict, but I have to, I know, to make a story. You gotta balance what they need with what the reader needs. But Zatz the problem. No readers. No thank you. No comment. No use. I raft the salty rapids of rejection but I got tossed up on shore one day and I was paralyzed. I couldn't write, which why don't you just pull a plastic bag over my head and tie it around my neck. Couldn't hear my people or see them and what will happen to them if I desert them? Except I hate them too because why can't they behave like people who would get me published?

But it's not their fault and it's not my fault, it's stores like this, publishers like this telling you what to want, not to think, not to feel. Where's my publisher? This is good material. *(Psssss)* I was suffocating, my people were suffocating. Writing's like my body, man. I gotta be able to breathe. Withdrawing just congealed my bile, like the bitter coffee at the bottom of the pot at the end of the day and we're still selling it. I drop it drop by drop in my cup, contain my rage, like people on the page, not harming anyone, or God forbid, any *objects*.

But then I stopped being able to *read*. Think about, readers. What if you couldn't look a page in the face because print is the rainbow pot, the end of a long trail of acceptance and support and confidence of other people in the work, while I perfect work for the closet, the attic, the filedrawer, the bonfire.

Just a minute, Officer. I know I got the right to remain silent. Also I got the right to speak. Jealousy's a heavy metal, man, gets in your system, hits your major organs, travels up you like a spinal tap and fries your brain. Couldn't write, couldn't read, couldn't feel. Did you ever jump around on your foot when it was asleep? Gotta slam it hard to wake it up. Least I got some feeling back. And you will not forget me. Zatz for sure.

Here I come. All I got is spraypaint. So frisk me.

No, I don't believe in lawyers. I'll defend myself. Ladies and gentlemen of the jury, Zatz my story. You decide. Should I be punished? Or should I be published?

They let you have paper in jail, right?

KALISHA. (*On the jobsite with a thermos-top coffee cup.*) I belong in this union. Ax any man I work wif. Some girls like workin' in bed. Some wanna be a model, or get dem a cushy gommint job. One time I was like dat. But someone gotta build. Might's well be me. I need stone. I need steel. I need to smell my sweat, mix it into concrete. Mixin' concrete—that's beauty. Remind me of time. Bitty rocks and chips like tough little mixed-up minutes flowin' into frames like time into plans. Harden into someplace you can live.

My man never made no plans. He spill out his time like a bad batch of concrete, like it wadn't worth nothin', left a big sloppy mess on the groun'. Take a sledgehammer to bust that up, I thought. He save me the trouble.

Yes, he work dis job befo' me. But he din' love dis job like I love dis job. I fought for dis job. Oh, dat handsome devil start out fine, then that cyclone of greed rip him up so fast, snatch bread out my babies' moufs. He smoking and selling and sleeping, say, "I ain't gonna do it, Kalisha, that slave labor."

"I know what you a slave to," I tell him. "My babies is my boss," I tell him. "I work for them if you won't." "I gotta go to Baltimore for one big score." And he gone, like steam off coffee. Alphonse tell me next time he don't show dey gwine fire his ass, so my little sister take my twins. I put dat hard hat on, I march down to dat site,

39

I said, "I am Sylvester today. You gimme somethin' to do." Sure,
they did laugh at me, but I lift up dat wheelbarrow six concrete
blocks inna basin, dey put me to work. Course, ten time dat day
dey make me lift dat barrow. Ten time a day for sixty-six days. Den
dey let me be. Hell, I lift my twins up fitty times a day.

'Bout four month later, most everybody gone, I'm on site, packin'
my belt, goin' pick up my twins and a pizza. Here come Sylvester
high as a skyscraper. Gotta blowtorch for a mouf' and aiming at
me. Call me ever name they is. Ax me what I'm doin there.
"Someone gotta build," I say. He say, "What you ever build?" "I
pour that slab you standin' on, for one thing." He jump off like his
feet on fire, pick him up a sledgehammer, starts to whackin' and
crackin' my slab. I get mad sometime how scared I get, but I get
scared sometime, how mad I get. "Set down dat sledge, Sylvester,
or this chisel find a home in your belly." He thow it down. I pick it
up. "I could smash you skull," I say, "but ain't in my plan. Time
like concrete, gotta pour it into some kinda shape to get use from
it. You a grown man, still don' know that? Beside, ain't my bid-
ness to give you your due. Just get you sorry ass away from me and
don' come round me or my babies again."

"You destroyin' me, Kalisha." "You doin' that youself, Sylvester."
"Kalisha, you think you build but you destroy." "Sylvester, when I
first begin to build, I was destroying in my mind. In my mind I
pour my concrete over your feet, lower the blocks over your greasy
head, cement your lyin' lips together. Lay your greedy body in the
walls. Sometime it sweet to hate so much. But den I come to like
the stone, the heaviness. This I can lift. This I can bear on ma back.
These ma muscles shinin' in the sun. Construction builds me. I can
lift a wheelbarrow now got eight blocks in. But I can't lift you,

baby."

Next thing I hear, Sylvester stoled him a backhoe off the site. Dug a ATM out the side of a bank, tried to bust it open. Didn't get noth-in'—the money goes into the bank a whole lot further than you think. Dey caught him bashin' it up on a chilren's playground.

But I been thinking about what he say. My momma name me for a powerful woman. Kali is the oldest Queen of Life, way back to India. She make, but she destroy. What this mean, I ax myself. What kinda truth last dat many years? I think about my babies I made, men I love, my friends, my little sister. Ain't nobody I love I ain't hurt. Ain't nobody love me never ain't me. Sad truth is we can't live without we hurtin' people.

So someone gotta build. Might's well be me. You know I belong in this union. I know I'm getting' in one day. I whisper my plans in the concrete.

AUDREY. (*To a class of young women.*) In eighty-one, before anyone had ever heard of Medugorje *(Pronounced Med-ju-gor-yay),* my fiancé and I were looking for a place for our wedding. We met a priest who looked like a carving of a Slavic saint. He declared the Virgin Mary was appearing to a group of shepherd children on a hillside in his homeland of Croatia. He invited us to travel with him, meet the children, and write about it for American newspapers. True or not, it jerked up my childhood, when my body and my faith were one. And every life should have one pilgrimage.

Though we were engaged, we got no time alone. Our pushy priest insisted, "Go here, meet them, no delay." Discomfort was provided in a wide array: shortslept nights, flies, hunger, no water after seven, no bathing for a week, the beating sun, true thirst, the ongoing abrasion of a foreign tongue.

Medugorje. When Our Lady began appearing to six children on a hillside, they told their pastor. He asked them to request that she appear at his church instead. And so she did, daily, for more than a year.

As we opened that wide wood door, our bodies and our faith were one again. We were keen.

Entering the vestibule, I felt a visceral revulsion. A life-sized star-

crowned plaster Mary was encircled by ancient black-babushka
women on their knees, groveling, a writhing wreathe of abasement.
My mind understood the devotion, but I was revolted, seeing
women beg, as they had begged and groveled this whole trip. My
body separated from my faith right then.

The priest pushed us through the throngs, to a room behind the
altar to witness, with the favored and the urgent few, the shepherd
children as they had their Vision. A room of faithfilled faces, teary
voices, bawling babies, shaking braces.

Passion in the prayer, in the air. We felt embarrassment and shame.
Among the ill, the injured and the lame we brought but damaged
faith.

With a perfect view of all six children's faces, we saw them seek
Her. All at once their features streamed with joy.

Six beatific children mesmerized, moving with a shared precision
that can't be simulated by the most sophisticated players much less
simple rural children. At once they loosed a passionate "Amen!"
that raised gooseflesh on my arms. I know they saw Her. I count it
still a profound privilege, to have breathed such rare air. Yet I'd felt
no change of temperature, no vibration, other energy. My body was
leaving my faith behind. I left limping, with a cane. I pitied the
women their faith and myself the loss of it.

Years passed. The murders, the bombs and the tortures began. We
wept for the people we'd met, tobacco-brown bodies, ancient mar-
ble cities rubbled, haunted by black-babushka women, scrubbing
the floor with their sorrow, chopping the stalks of their anguish,

suckling death at dry breasts. To lose faith—it is not so bad as losing a hand, a home, a child. Besides, if faith cannot prevent a holocaust what good is it? Even if they saw Her, and I believe they did, even if millions of Americans have visited, and they have, even if rosaries have turned from silver to gold, and my aunt has shown me hers, what does it matter when blood runs down the street?

Live without faith until your body quakes with truth.

I heard of a woman who stayed in Croatia to report on the massacres for Human Rights Watch. The soldiers told her "Leave." She stayed, and wrote her notes. They raped her. She stayed and wrote her notes. They beat her husband, tore apart her house. She stayed, and wrote her notes. So someone would know what happened, she said.

She is my vision on a hillside. She was not keeping faith, defending faith, like it was some goblet at the Vatican that once it's lost it's gone. She was birthing faith, out of her hands, her eyes, between her legs, and there is my miracle. Think about what you consecrate your life to. Go forth and give birth.

JORDY. Did you know you can fill a room with your joy? Did you know this is what people really want? Movement is the first commandment. You owe it to your body to obey it. Dancin' is the hymnal:

Fingers flinging alleluias. Torso folding lamentation. Fierce, dance fierce, then light, like a swimmer skimming water. I might could tell you things more mysterious: How one body tells another it is beautiful. How the grace of flesh, physicality, the power of creation drip like spangles from your moving arm. And how you cannot hold to ecstasy, for ecstasy will crowd you out upon itself. These things I can tell you as certainly as worship, but I cannot tell you them in words.

Did you know it don't matter what happened when you was a child? You cannot hold to grievance for grievance will crowd you out upon itself. It will ice your body up, stop up your sap, truss up yourself like a old turkey. Where is them spangles now?

You got something to say, you stomp your history out across a floor. Pound on Mama Earth. She glad to hear from you. She can take it all. And your own limbs can answer any question put to them.

You wanna blame someone? Blame yourself for forgetting what's going on right now. The beauty of *this* world.

And don't you tell me I don't know what grief is. I dance my drunk Daddy. I dance my dead daughter.

Free ain't somethin' you get when you buy somethin'. It's a psalm you sing yourself.

Remember you can fill a room with your joy. Remember this is what *you* really want.

PRODUCTION NOTES

WOMEN ON FIRE is a series of portraits, performed by one extremely versatile actress, or several. As such, it is performed with the simplest of sets. A roll of photographer's paper serves as backdrop for a simple wooden chair with arms, which becomes waiting room chair, confessional, sickbed, bookstore ladder, and so on. For some portraits *(Elizabeth, for example)* it is disregarded altogether.

SOUND and LIGHTS:
Change of character and scene is implied by transitional music and lights. An occasional flash and sound of camera shutter punctuates the end of some pieces, to remind us these are portraits. The music used in the New York production was selections from "The T'ao of Cello" by David Darling.

COSTUME:
Simple, basic black with eyeglasses, scarf, garden hat, etc. signifying character change.

PROPS are only those easily carried on and off by hand:
    Cellphone [Trade]
    Small kitten cross-stich or crewel piece *(in progress)* [Fern]
    Cigarette *(unlit)* [Clover]
    Hand-held tape recorder [Lydia]
    Wineglass [Lydia]
    Dacquiri glass [Miriam]
    Spray can [Zatz] *(For the effect of spraypaint with no muss and no fuss, use a can of compressed air such as is used to clean computer keyboards)*
    Thermos-top coffee-cup [Kalisha]

WHITE BUFFALO
Don Zolidis

Drama / 3m, 2f (plus chorus)/ Unit Set

Based on actual events, WHITE BUFFALO tells the story of the miracle birth of a white buffalo calf on a small farm in southern Wisconsin. When Carol Gelling discovers that one of the buffalo on her farm is born white in color, she thinks nothing more of it than a curiosity. Soon, however, she learns that this is the fulfillment of an ancient prophecy believed by the Sioux to bring peace on earth and unity to all mankind. Her little farm is quickly overwhelmed with religious pilgrims, bringing her into contact with a culture and faith that is wholly unfamiliar to her. When a mysterious businessman offers to buy the calf for two million dollars, Carol is thrown into doubt about whether to profit from the religious beliefs of others or to keep true to a spirituality she knows nothing about.

SKIN DEEP
Jon Lonoff

Comedy / 2m, 2f / Interior Unit Set

In *Skin Deep*, a large, lovable, lonely-heart, named Maureen Mulligan, gives romance one last shot on a blind-date with sweet awkward Joseph Spinelli; she's learned to pepper her speech with jokes to hide insecurities about her weight and appearance, while he's almost dangerously forthright, saying everything that comes to his mind. They both know they're perfect for each other, and in time they come to admit it.

They were set up on the date by Maureen's sister Sheila and her husband Squire, who are having problems of their own: Sheila undergoes a non-stop series of cosmetic surgeries to hang onto the attractive and much-desired Squire, who may or may not have long ago held designs on Maureen, who introduced him to Sheila. With Maureen particularly vulnerable to both hurting and being hurt, the time is ripe for all these unspoken issues to bubble to the surface.

"Warm-hearted comedy ... the laughter was literally show-stopping. A winning play, with enough good-humored laughs and sentiment to keep you smiling from beginning to end."
- TalkinBroadway.com

"It's a little Paddy Chayefsky, a lot Neil Simon and a quick-witted, intelligent voyage into the not-so-tranquil seas of middle-aged love and dating. The dialogue is crackling and hilarious; the plot simple but well-turned; the characters endearing and quirky; and lurking beneath the merriment is so much heartache that you'll stand up and cheer when the unlikely couple makes it to the inevitable final clinch."
- NYTheatreWorld.Com

THE OFFICE PLAYS
Two full length plays by Adam Bock

THE RECEPTIONIST
Comedy / 2m, 2f / Interior

At the start of a typical day in the Northeast Office, Beverly deals effortlessly with ringing phones and her colleague's romantic troubles. But the appearance of a charming rep from the Central Office disrupts the friendly routine. And as the true nature of the company's business becomes apparent, The Receptionist raises disquieting, provocative questions about the consequences of complicity with evil.

"...Mr. Bock's poisoned Post-it note of a play."
- New York Times

"Bock's intense initial focus on the routine goes to the heart of *The Receptionist's* pointed, painfully timely allegory... elliptical, provocative play..."
- Time Out New York

THE THUGS
Comedy / 2m, 6f / Interior

The Obie Award winning dark comedy about work, thunder and the mysterious things that are happening on the 9th floor of a big law firm. When a group of temps try to discover the secrets that lurk in the hidden crevices of their workplace, they realize they would rather believe in gossip and rumors than face dangerous realities.

"Bock starts you off giggling, but leaves you with a chill."
- Time Out New York

"... a delightfully paranoid little nightmare that is both more chillingly realistic and pointedly absurd than anything John Grisham ever dreamed up."
- New York Times

SAMUELFRENCH.COM

BLUE YONDER
Kate Aspengren

Dramatic Comedy / Monolgues and scenes
12f (can be performed with as few as 4 with doubling) / Unit Set

A familiar adage states, "Men may work from sun to sun, but women's work is never done." In Blue Yonder, the audience meets twelve mesmerizing and eccentric women including a flight instructor, a firefighter, a stuntwoman, a woman who donates body parts, an employment counselor, a professional softball player, a surgical nurse professional baseball player, and a daredevil who plays with dynamite among others. Through the monologues, each woman examines her life's work and explores the career that she has found. Or that has found her.

CPSIA information can be obtained
at www.ICGtesting.com
Printed in the USA
LVOW13s2340120217
524076LV00029B/1168/P